Scott Foresman

Readers' Theater Anthology

Editorial Offices: Glenview, Illinois • Parsippany, New Jersey • New York, New York
Sales Offices: Needham, Massachusetts • Duluth, Georgia • Glenview, Illinois
Coppell, Texas • Sacramento, California • Mesa, Arizona

Acknowledgments

Poetry

- **P4** "Idaho" from *A Snail's Failure Socially* by Kaye Starbird. Copyright © 1966 by Kaye Starbird.
- **P5** "Monday!" from *Somebody Catch My Homework!* by David L. Harrison. Copyright © 1993 by David L. Harrison. Published by Boyds Mills Press.
- **P6** "The Seed" by Aileen Fisher
- **P8** "The Mysterious Smirkle" from *Juggling with Gerbils* by Brian Patten, Puffin. Copyright © Brian Patten 2000.
- **P11** "Moonwalker" from *Lunch Money And Other Poems About School* by Carol Diggery Shields. Text copyright © 1995 by Carol Diggery Shields. Published by Dutton Children's Books a division of Penguin Books USA.
- **P12** "To Dark Eyes Dreaming" from *Today is Saturday* by Zilpha Keatley Snyder. Copyright © 1969 by Zilpha Keatley Snyder. Published by Atheneum.
- **P13** "A Summer Morning" from *The Pointed People* by Rachel Field. Published by the Macmillan Company.
- **P15** "74th Street" from *The Malibu and Other Poems* by Myra Cohn Livingston. Copyright © 1972 by Myra Cohn Livingston. Reprinted by permission of Marian Reiner for the author.

ISBN: 0-328-14732-X

Copyright © Pearson Education, Inc.

All Rights Reserved. Printed in the United States of America. This publication, or parts thereof, may be used with appropriate equipment to reproduce copies for classroom use only.

1 2 3 4 5 6 7 8 9 10 V004 09 08 07 06 05

Contents

Practice with a Purpose by Sam Sebesta iv
Readers' Theater in Your Classroom by Alisha Fran-Potter vi
About the Playwrights xii

Unit 1 This Land Is Your Land
D. C. Riddle Rally by Cynthia Gallaher

Unit 2 Work and Play
The Boy Who Would Be Famous by Marie Yuen

Unit 3 Patterns in Nature
Stories for a Starry Night by Peter Grahame

Unit 4 Puzzles and Mysteries
The Twelve Dancing Princesses by Alisha Fran-Potter

Unit 5 Adventures by Land, Air, and Water
To Go with the Flow by Susan DiLallo

Unit 6 Reaching for Goals
Carla's Race by Amy Fellner Dominy

Poetry
Poetry Interpretation P1
Poetry P4
Tests About Poetry P13

Practice with a Purpose

by Sam Sebesta

As indicated in the directions in this book, Readers' Theater is a performance activity with a simple format. Costumes, makeup, and scenery are not required. Action is minimal. Because scripts are used, there's no lengthy time spent memorizing lines.

The goal is a shared oral reading performance that rocks the rafters, whether an audience is present or not. People with long memories compare it to radio drama in days of old. Yet there's nothing out-of-date about Readers' Theater. Its benefits are recognized by modern researchers. Listen to this:

ABOUT THE AUTHOR
Sam Sebesta is a Professor Emeritus from the College of Education at the University of Washington in Seattle. He continues to write and do research in children's literature, decoding in linguistic development, oral reading fluency, and reader response.

TEACHER *(puzzled):* Why are we doing Readers' Theater?

READING PROFESSOR *(reading from a scholarly paper):* "Readers' Theater promotes fluency and expression as a result of repeated reading and encouragement to make the performance sound natural and meaningful."

STUDENT *(aside):* Will that be on the test?

No, that won't be on the test, although it's a good rationale for teachers to know about. Beyond this, it might be beneficial to discuss the reasons for Readers' Theater with your class.

TEACHER *(still puzzled):* Why are we doing Readers' Theater?

STUDENT 1: Because it's fun.

STUDENT 2: Because you learn to get the words right.

STUDENT 3: You learn to speak up so others can hear you.

STUDENT 4 *(the reflective one):* It's good for the imagination.

Good reasons, all. Here are five more, gleaned from comments during Readers' Theater classes and workshops:

"You get practice with a purpose."

The purpose, of course, is to present a worthy performance. The practice? It begins the moment scripts are passed out. It continues as students take their "parts" home or to a quiet corner to practice their lines. It flourishes in group rehearsal.

"You learn to make it sound like people talking."

A smooth delivery—flow of language, not word-by-word—is an objective in Readers' Theater that students can understand. How to achieve it? Practice reading a line and then look up and say it directly to another character. Pretty soon the fluency will come.

"More of you get to read at one time."

In this student's class, several groups are rehearsing their scripts simultaneously before they come together to perform for each other. The ratio of readers to listeners is higher than you'd find in classes where one reads and all others listen. Hence, there's more practice, more involvement.

"You learn to get into character."

Sounds too grown-up? Not at all! Children realize, from the start, that the way to portray Chicken Little is to try running like Chicken Little and talking like Chicken Little. Using mime and made-up speeches to help "get into character" may be a useful device to prepare for Readers' Theater. And there may be a more lasting payoff: readers who enjoy reading often see themselves in the roles of the characters they're reading about.

"It's reading you get to do with your friends."

Avid readers, when interviewed, speak frequently about the social value of reading, praising reading activities that have them interacting with peers. Non-avid readers who think of reading as a lonely task may also find that interactive activities such as Readers' Theater and Choral Reading alter attitudes toward the positive.

These, then, are benefits you may discover from Readers' Theater and Choral Reading. There may be more. The effects of good oral reading may be internalized, resulting in improved silent reading. Hence, speaking and listening to complex style, dialogue in character, and other features of print contribute to effective silent reading. It's no coincidence that avid readers (i.e., children and young adults who read voluntarily an hour or more a day) cite reading aloud and being read to as the major factor leading to their success.

With all these reasons in mind, Scott Foresman Reading Street offers you the directions and selections in this book. We hope you enjoy them. We want you to find them useful as a component of a powerful reading program.

Readers' Theater in Your Classroom

by Alisha Fran-Potter

Staging the Play

ACTING AREA

If you don't have a stage at your disposal, your classroom will work fine. First you need to define a functional acting area. This could be the front or back of the room with some or all of the desks pushed out of the way. It could be a taped-off area on the floor. If you need or want to leave all your desks in place, you will need enough space in front of the room for students to stand in a row. Once you decide what will work best for your class and room layout, explain to your students and train them how to prepare the acting area when you give the signal.

ABOUT THE AUTHOR
Alisha Fran-Potter is a Drama Specialist with the Glenview, Illinois public schools. She has taught in classrooms at grades K, 1, and 2, and speech, drama, and language arts at grades 6, 7, and 8.

MOVEMENT AND BLOCKING

Traditionally, Readers' Theater is performed with the actors seated on chairs or stools in a row facing the audience, with their scripts in their hands or on stands in front of them. Actors do not memorize their parts but read them or at least refer to their scripts as they act. In this traditional method, actors do not look at each other but keep their focus out front. You can include movement in your production or not. Decide before you start how much movement there will be. Keep in mind that if students have scripts in their hands, their movements must be limited. If they remain in place, they might gesture with one free hand.

Any movement about the stage you have the actors do is called *blocking*. Your blocking choices depend on your acting area. If you have the space and want to have your actors move about freely, do so. However, if your acting area is limited, keep the blocking simple, perhaps just having the actors move from one chair to another, cross the stage, or come and go in the acting area.

If the actors are up and moving around, you need to consider their focus (whom they are talking to), and angle (the direction they face). Actors should not face each other directly, but rather turn their bodies slightly toward the audience. This is called *cheating,* and if done well it can look perfectly natural. In cheating positions, two actors would position their bodies at about 90° to each other.

If there is a place that remains the same throughout the story, such as a house or a lake, you might tape an area out on the floor or block it off with chairs or markers. This way all actors know where the place is within the acting area. You can designate entrances and exits in the same way.

ENTRANCES AND EXITS

For a smooth-running performance, rehearse entrances and exits when you rehearse the play.

- Actors can all enter at the same time, go to their assigned places, and then all exit at the same time. Or, they can all be "discovered" by lights up at the beginning—with lights down to signal the end.
- Actors can enter as their characters come into the story and then stay or leave and come back. You will need to decide if all the actors stay on stage after their parts are finished. (If they remain, they can all share a curtain call.)
- Actors can remain at their desks until it is their turn to perform, do their roles, and then go back to their seats. This works only if your classroom is big enough to accommodate a seating area and separate acting area.

ASSIGNING PARTS

Plan in advance how parts will be assigned and explain the process to your students. Some ways to do this are:

Volunteers This method allows students to volunteer for the parts they are interested in. Go though all the parts and describe them if necessary. Then explain that when you ask who is interested in playing each part they should raise their hands. Suggest that students have second and third choices in mind because they won't always get their first choices. If you know that a volunteer can't handle a specific part for whatever reason, choose another student and give the first student a more appropriate part. This works better with some groups than with other groups, and you must assess your students' abilities to handle volunteering.

Draw Markers To assign parts randomly, make up sticks with the student's names on them. Choose a stick and assign that person the part that is up next. This works well if all the parts are about the same in length and ability—and if the parts are gender-neutral. You will have to use your discretion, however, to avoid choosing a student who can't handle the reading of a role because it is large or because it will embarrass the student for some reason.

Introduction **vii**

Teacher Choice Do this ahead of time to save class time. Simply go through the cast list and the student list and decide who will play what part. This works well—and indeed may be necessary—if there are varied abilities in the class and the roles vary much in length. But you must know your students and the parts in the play well in order to use this method.

Audition The audition choice is new to your students in fourth grade. You may want to run practice auditions before you actually hold one. Students can do a cold reading from the script, or they can be given time to prepare. Preparation time could vary from five minutes to a class period or the next day. Depending on the abilities of the students, you can choose the passages for audition or let the students choose. This method works if you have a large amount of time for the play or a number of periods for preparation and rehearsal.

SCENERY AND PROPS

Scenery provides the *setting*—where the story takes place. If you have access to a curtain backdrop, use it by all means. Chances are, however, that you are stuck with a wall of your classroom. If you have the space, you might be able to arrange desks, tables, carts, easels, chairs, and so on to suggest a setting. You might consider having students create a scene in colored chalk on your chalkboard. Keep in mind, however, that the best scenery is created in the imaginations of your audience.

Props are anything the actors handle. Traditional Readers' Theater uses no props, but if you choose to use props, keep them simple. Remember that the actors still have to manipulate their scripts. If the play calls for a bag or a purse, the actor can use a backpack or coat. Other ordinary classroom items that can serve as props include: books, clipboards, pencil cases, boxes, book ends, pens or pencils, paper, note cards, notebooks, cups, vases, water bottles.

Adapting Scripts

Ideally, every student in a class or group will have his or her own role in Readers' Theater. If these scripts have too many or too few roles for your class, you may need to adapt them to fit. To reduce characters:

- Eliminate parts that are redundant or not vital to the plot. For example, reduce four narrators to two by having Narrator 1 read lines designated Narrator 1 and Narrator 3, and so on.

- Take out parts with animal sounds or cheering crowds and just let the audience infer them.

- Characters with single lines or few lines can be doubled by actors who aren't in the same scene.

- Perform only scenes for which you have enough actors. You can summarize or narrate missing scenes that are needed to get the story across.

To add characters:

- If there are many Narrator lines, divide them up to allow for more narrators.
- Have two students play a role at the same time. If there is a cat in the story, turn it into two cats. They can alternate lines or recite them in unison.
- Add a counterpart character and have them say their lines together or divide the lines. For example, if there is a Queen in the story, create a King.
- If there is a part such as Townsperson, turn it into Townspeople and have more than one actor read it simultaneously.
- If many extra parts are needed, cast by scene. For example, have different actors play the King in Scene 1 and Scene 2.

Note that the suggestions for simultaneous reading also work well to help students with special needs or ELL students who are just learning English.

Adapting Trade Books for Readers' Theater

You can adapt any kind of book into a Readers' Theater script. But not every story is equally suited to the stage. Look for a story with a strong narrative line. An easy-to-follow plot adapts more effectively than a plot or story line that is too complex. If it feels complicated, you might need to simplify the plot somehow. Even nonfiction books can be turned into scripts, but among those, the books with strong narrative lines—such as biography or history—will be most effective. Here are some further elements to consider:

Narration When you are adapting your script, first eliminate all speech tags, such as "he said" and "Josefina replied." Eliminate lengthy descriptions. If you feel some description is necessary, try to put it in the mouth of a character who has a reason to describe something.

Narrators can be very useful, but try to keep their function to introducing, enhancing, or moving the story along. Sometimes they may be necessary to make transitions between scenes. However, don't rely on narrators to tell the story. For example, don't write:

NARRATOR: It is early Monday morning. Mary is eagerly waiting for friends to look at her garden before the judges come. Finally Tessa arrives.

MARY: I'll show you my flowers.

NARRATOR: Together they walk to the garden in back of the house. They see beautiful bright yellow sunflowers and blazing red poppies.

Aim to show, not to tell. In other words, dramatize, don't narrate. For example, you might write:

NARRATOR: It is early Monday morning. Mary is eagerly waiting.

MARY: Good morning, Tessa!

TESSA: Hi, Mary. I've come to see that award-winning garden of yours.

MARY: I hope. But I'm glad you could come before the judges get here.

TESSA: So am I. I can't wait to see what you've done this year. I hear it's beautiful and full of color.

MARY: Oh, it is! I have bright yellow sunflowers and blazing red poppies. Here, let me show you. It's out back. Follow me.

You will find that it is helpful to have characters repeat each other's names often. This helps the audience keep track of who is speaking, especially when there are a lot of characters in a scene.

Dialogue Look at the dialogue in a book to see how much there is. Some dialogue you might be able to use directly in your script. Some you may need to simplify or pare down. Some dialogue you may decide to break up into smaller units, so that one character doesn't talk for too long at one time.

Be sure that the dialogue is appropriate for the age group you're working with. If not, you may be able to make it more appropriate by cutting or substituting some words or phrases.

If you are creating new dialogue, be sure it is in the voice of the character; that is, appropriate to that character's age, education, sophistication, and so on.

Repetition Repetition may be of actions or of language. Repetition of actions allows actors—and the audience—to follow the story line more easily. For example, the First Pig builds a house of straw, the Second Pig builds a house of twigs, and the Third Pig builds a house of bricks.

Repetition of language might be a repeated phrase or sentence such as the Wolf's line, "I'll huff and I'll puff and I'll blow your house down!" which he says before his attack on each Pig's house.

Younger children especially do well with repetition, but don't discount its effectiveness even for the older grades. Many elaborate folk tales develop their plot lines through the use of repetition.

Group Characters These allow for multiple roles. For example, if you have twenty-six actors with one main character and five supporting characters, all can have a role. One or two actors can play the main character, and then several actors can play each of the supporting characters. For example, take the story *Anansi and the Moss-Covered Rock* by Eric Kimmel.

X   Introduction

Anansi, the spider, is walking though the forest when he finds a magic rock. He uses this rock to trick his friends so he can take their food. Little Bush Deer won't let Anansi fool him, though, and teaches Anansi a lesson in turn.

One or two actors can play Anansi, one or two can play the rock, and the rest of the actors can be divided among the other animals. So you might have three or four Lions, Elephants, Rhinoceroses, Hippopotamuses, Giraffes, Zebras, and Little Bush Deers.

Special Effects

You can create effective Readers' Theater using nothing but the actors' voices. However, if you want to add to the theatrical experience, consider the following:

MUSIC

You can use recorded or live music (such as a piano or guitar) to make transitions between scenes, to show the passage of time, or for background to heighten the mood. Be sure that the music is appropriate to the mood and pace of the scene. If you are using recorded music, practice cueing it up during rehearsals.

LIGHTING

If you are working on a stage with a lighting system, you can either open the curtain or bring the lights up on your actors already in place. If the actors must take their places in view of the audience, you can dim the lights to black and then bring them up to signal the start of the performance.

SOUND EFFECTS

Remember that the actors themselves can create all the sound effects with their voices alone. However, here are some additional suggestions for these plays.

The Boy Who Would Be Famous The sound effects are minimal. A sound effects person can vocally imitate a baby crying. Any actor knocking on any wood surface will serve for the door knocks, and two or three actors can contribute the polite clapping.

To Go with the Flow The carpenter's hammering can be accomplished simply by pounding with a block on any wood surface. The farm animals can be done vocally by one or more sound-effects people. Students might experiment with various classroom objects that can be smashed together to create the boat collisions.

About the Playwrights

Cynthia Gallaher studied screenwriting and also studied oral interpretation at St. Nicholas Theater Company. She wrote the script for the mini-musical "Can't Help But Dance" in Theatre Building Chicago Writers' Workshop. She was awarded a Community Arts Assistance Program Grant in Theater from the City of Chicago, and she is currently writing the book and lyrics for a children's musical, *Xavier and the White Cat.*

Marie Yuen has appeared onstage in Hong Kong and Chicago. In China she won a short story competition and an acting award. She is a member of Chicago Dramatists Workshop, Theatre Building Chicago Writers' Workshop, and the Dramatists Guild. Her plays *Silk Scarf* and *My Father's Father* were produced in Chicago. She wrote the book for the musical *Too Many Cooks*, which was workshopped and produced in Chicago.

Peter Grahame has written Readers' Theater scripts for community projects as well as educational materials for young people. He has acted in or directed community, academic, and professional theatrical productions in many cities across the country. He is also an artist and a photographer. His short play "In Search of Wisdom" was published in a reading textbook.

Alisha Fran-Potter is a Drama Specialist with Glenview (IL) School District 34. She has her BS in Education and her Masters in Curriculum and Instruction, with an emphasis in Fine Arts. She has taught Kindergarten, 1st and 2nd grade, Drama for K–8, and 6-7-8-grade Drama and Speech. Mrs. Fran-Potter developed, wrote, and implemented fine arts curriculums for Districts 34 and 81. She has presented at the Illinois Reading Council and taught for Glenview University.

Susan DiLallo wrote a humor column for the Rye, New York *Record*. She won the Kleban and the Richard Rodgers Awards to develop her musical *Once Upon a Time in New Jersey,* which was workshopped and produced in Allentown, Pennsylvania. She also won the Hangar Theatre KIDDSTUFF New Play Competition for her book and lyrics to *Pinocchio*. Her further credits include *That's Life, This Week in the Suburbs*, and *A Christmas Valentine.*

Amy Fellner Dominy writes for both children's theater and adult theater. She studied creative writing at Arizona State University. A number of her plays have had readings or productions, among them *The Bathtub, The Dreamcatcher, Oy! It's a Boy, Folding Memories, Some Assembly Required,* and *Plastic Angels.* She is a member of The Dramatists Guild, the Society of Children's Book Writers, and the Association of Jewish Theatre.

D.C. Riddle Rally

BY CYNTHIA GALLAHER

CHARACTERS

MRS. JOHNSON, Teacher
MR. SLATER, Bus Driver
MR. ESCOBAR, Parent Chaperone
MRS. PARELLO, Parent Chaperone
MARIA (10 years)
RICKY (9 years)
BECKY (9 years)
NATE (9 years)
JOE (9 years)
TARA (10 years)
ELENA (10 years)
FRANK (9 years)
NARRATORS 1–4

WITH HELP FROM A RIDDLE
CHALLENGE A FOURTH-GRADE CLASS
FINDS THAT LEARNING ABOUT
THE NATION'S CAPITAL
CAN BE LOTS OF FUN!

SCENE 1

BECKY Aren't we there yet, Mrs. Johnson? We've been on the bus for an hour.

MRS. JOHNSON Well, Becky, Mr. Slater is making sure he doesn't go faster than the speed limit. But let's ask him. Mr. Slater, how much longer?

MR. SLATER We'll be in Washington in just a few minutes, kids.

NARRATOR 1 Mrs. Johnson's fourth-grade class is taking a class trip to Washington, D.C., on a beautiful spring day. Now it's time for Mrs. Johnson and the two parent chaperones on the bus—Mrs. Parello and Mr. Escobar—to tell about the surprise they have worked up for the kids.

MRS. JOHNSON Now class, let's talk about the Riddle Rally.

RICKY What's a Riddle Rally?

MRS. JOHNSON Mr. Escobar, would you like to answer Ricky's question?

MR. ESCOBAR Sure, Mrs. Johnson. I'll be glad to. Kids, we've worked up a riddle challenge for you. All day, you'll be answering riddles about the places we visit.

MRS. PARELLO That's right, Mr. Escobar. Before we make each stop, our teams will have a chance to solve a riddle about it.

MR. ESCOBAR Thanks, Mrs. Parello. And of course, there will be prizes to be won.

MRS. JOHNSON Students, remember the teams we talked about? Each pair of students sitting together is a team. And each team has a color name—the same as the color on your nametag. You teams will solve the riddles and write your answers on the index cards I'll pass out. Then I'll take them up.

FRANK Mrs. Johnson, what are the prizes?

MRS. JOHNSON That's a surprise, Frank! Now class, how about a punctuation lesson?

ALL STUDENTS *(ad lib)* Awwh! Ick! That's no good! C'mon!

BECKY I thought today was supposed to be fun, Mrs. Johnson.

MRS. JOHNSON But, Becky, punctuation has everything to do with the first riddle. Mr. Escobar? Mrs. Parello? Please give us the riddle.

MRS. PARELLO A sight like this will never disappoint.

MR. ESCOBAR Because the place looks like an exclamation point!

MRS. PARELLO Some call it handsome, and some say it's pretty,

MR. ESCOBAR And people look at it all over the city.

RICKY *(whispering)* An exclamation point comes at the end of a sentence, just like a period does, Maria.

MARIA *(whispering)* Yeah, Ricky, it looks like a ballbat with a dot underneath. And you use it when you want your sentence to sound like a shout.

ELENA *(calling out)* I think we're in Washington, D. C., now!

RICKY *(whispering)* And look, I see our exclamation point over there!

MARIA Oh, Ricky, I think you just got the answer! I'll write it down.

NARRATOR 2 The teams of students turn in their answers to Mrs. Johnson.

MRS. JOHNSON Do I have all the cards now? Okay, Mrs. Parello, the answer?

MRS. PARELLO It's the Washington Monument, the tall white obelisk structure that you see out the window.

TARA Mrs. Johnson, what is a Bob . . . makes a . . . fist . . . ?

MRS. JOHNSON You mean an obelisk? It's a tall four-sided shape with a little pyramid on top. Just like the shape of the Washington Monument.

MR. SLATER You know, that thing helps me remember which direction I'm driving when I'm in Washington, because I can see it from anywhere in the city.

D. C. Riddle Rally

MRS. PARELLO But before we get there, we have another riddle. Mr. Escobar?

MR. ESCOBAR When you name the place where our bus next stops,

MRS. PARELLO It sounds like it's a row of shops,

MR. ESCOBAR There are no windows, you'll find no door,

MRS. PARELLO And the length of it has a grassy floor.

FRANK Why are you giving us two riddles in a row?

MR. ESCOBAR Because the first riddle fits into the second riddle.

NARRATOR 3 The teams work on the riddle, then turn in their cards.

MRS. JOHNSON Okay, students. The answer is the Mall, the park where the Washington Monument is located.

SCENE 2

NARRATOR 4 The students get off the bus, walk through the pathways of the Mall, and take the elevator to the top of the Washington Monument.

BECKY Look how far you can see!

NATE Wow! It's like being in an airplane.

ELENA There's the White House! I know, because I see it on TV.

MRS. JOHNSON All right class. Wait in line to take the elevator back down.

NARRATOR 1 When the class is gathered at ground level again, Mrs. Johnson tells them they have another riddle to solve. She asks Mrs. Parello to start the riddle.

MRS. PARELLO A light-hearted crew thought to do something nice,

MR. ESCOBAR They walked through a strange land and brought back a slice.

MRS. PARELLO Now this slice shares a room with a four-sided kite,

MR. ESCOBAR And it sits underneath something crafted by Wright.

4 Unit 1 • This Land Is Your Land

NARRATOR 2 The students gather into their teams and write their answers.

MRS JOHNSON I have all the cards. Would one of you students like to tell the answer? Yes, Ricky?

RICKY The "slice" in the riddle is a piece of moon rock, and the Wright Brothers made and flew the first airplane.

MARIA They're both in the National Air and Space Museum, right?

MRS. JOHNSON *(laughing)* You may not be Wright—but you're right!

NARRATOR 3 The museum is a big hit with the kids. They gaze in wonder at the Wright 1903 Flyer, a real moon rock, and the first rocket plane to break the sound barrier. Too soon for some, they have to return to the bus.

MRS. JOHNSON Now we're headed to a monument on the other side of the Mall. Riddle tellers, take it away!

MR. ESCOBAR It takes only one red cent,

MRS. PARELLO To see where our next hour is spent.

MR. ESCOBAR On one side you can see the face,

MRS. PARELLO The other side, you'll find the place.

BECKY Nate. Quick, what kind of change do you have in your pockets?

NATE A few dimes and a nickel. But isn't the riddle talking about a penny?

MRS. JOHNSON Time's up. Cards, please . . . Now, who knows the answer?

JOE I do! The Lincoln Memorial.

FRANK How did you get that, Joe?

JOE I picked up a penny from the floor of the bus.

TARA Abraham Lincoln's picture is on one side of the penny.

JOE And the building we're pulling up to right now is on the other side.

D. C. Riddle Rally

SCENE 3

MRS. JOHNSON Here we are—the Lincoln Memorial. You know, Martin Luther King, Jr., gave his famous "I Have a Dream" speech right here in front of the memorial.

BECKY And I remember reading that Marian Anderson gave a concert here when they wouldn't let her sing in Constitution Hall because she was black.

NARRATOR 4 The students walk between the building's great columns to see an enormous statue of Abraham Lincoln seated in a chair facing the city.

ELENA Lincoln was our Civil War President. We studied about that last month. When he looks out over Washington today, I wonder if he likes what he sees?

NARRATOR 1 Back on the bus, the students are ready for another riddle.

MRS. PARELLO On the north side, you'll find two from each state.

MR. ESCOBAR On the south side, that's where hundreds debate.

MRS. PARELLO This white building sits up high on a hill.

MR. ESCOBAR It's where law starts, in the form of a bill.

JOE (whispering) This one is hard, Tara!

TARA Is it the White House, Joe?

MRS. JOHNSON Time's up. Cards, please! (Pause.) Well, I see that most of the teams got this one. But here's one that answered "White House." That's not correct—it's the Capitol.

TARA What's the difference, Mrs. Johnson? Isn't the Capitol the same as the White House?

MRS. PARELLO No, Tara. The President lives in the White House. Congress meets in the Capitol to make laws.

MRS. JOHNSON And I know this is confusing, but the Capitol building is spelled with an *O-L*, but when you refer to Washington, D.C., as our nations capital, that's spelled *A-L*.

MRS. ESCOBAR Everybody off the bus now. In good order, please!

SCENE 4

NARRATOR 2 The students climb the Capitol steps and enter the rotunda, a space under the big dome in the center of the building.

MRS. JOHNSON Senators in the north building and Representatives in the south building vote on bills to make our nation's laws. There are two Senators from every state, but there are hundreds of Representatives.

NARRATOR 3 After a history-packed tour of the Capitol, the class returns to the parking lot and gets on the bus.

MR. SLATER Welcome back, kids. Guess what? I found out what the prize is.

FRANK What is it, Mr. Slater?

MRS. JOHNSON *(laughing)* Mr. Slater won't tell, Frank. You have to solve this riddle too.

MRS. PARELLO They're all made from mint, but you can't taste it,

MR. ESCOBAR They all could be spent, but why ever waste it?

MRS. PARELLO One is a fourth and the whole's five times ten,

MR. ESCOBAR And on each is the first of a man among men.

NARRATOR 4 The teams talk among themselves and hand in cards again.

NARRATOR 1 Mrs. Johnson takes up the cards and tallies the results.

MRS. JOHNSON The prize is sets of the fifty new state quarters produced by the U. S. Mint. So Blue and Green teams, how did you figure it out?

NATE I know that when coins are made, they "mint" them, Mrs. Johnson.

BECKY And the one that is a fourth is a quarter. One fourth of a dollar.

D. C. Riddle Rally

NATE And five times ten is fifty. There are fifty states. So—fifty new state quarters. One for each state.

MARIA And George Washington, our first president, is on the front of each quarter.

MRS. JOHNSON Excellent. We have two complete sets of quarters for the winning team. But since you all worked so hard, you'll each get some newly minted quarters from the State Quarters set.

MR. ESCOBAR AND MRS. PARELLO Congratulations, everyone!

ALL *(ad lib)* Hooray! That was fun! Thanks!

MRS. JOHNSON Students, we're finished with our riddles, but before we head home, our bus driver, Mr. Slater, has a rap for you.

MR. SLATER From antique planes to presidents,
This city puts on quite a show,
Hope you'll come back, but now it's time,
To buckle up, 'cause here we go.

You kids all love to ride this bus,
Because it takes you far from school,
But you got more than just a trip,
You figured out that learning's cool!

The Boy Who Would Be Famous

The early years of Hans Christian Andersen
Marie Yuen

Poor young Hans has a dream of greatness and pursues that dream against all odds and hardships.

CHARACTERS

MRS. ANNE MARIE ANDERSEN
MR. HANS ANDERSEN
HANS
DAGMAR, Mrs. Andersen's Helper
MR. VILHELM NIELSEN, a Neighbor
MRS. GERTA RASMUSSEN, a Neighbor
LARS, a Factory Worker
SOREN, a Factory Worker
NIELS, a Classmate
MATILDE, a Classmate
GUNNAR, a Classmate
MADAME DURGA, a Fortuneteller
NARRATORS 1–4
SOUND EFFECTS

SCENE 1

SOUND EFFECTS *(Sound of a baby crying.)*

MRS. ANDERSEN There, there, little one. Look, here's your Momma. And your Poppa, too!

MR. ANDERSEN Such a tiny boy—

MRS. ANDERSEN And such a big name—Hans Christian Andersen.

MR. ANDERSEN I promise you, Anne Marie, he won't go hungry. For soon I'll have my own shoemaker shop and—

MRS. ANDERSEN And then life will be sunshine and roses! Yes, Hans. I know . . . though perhaps until then might I keep my work as a laundress?

MR. ANDERSEN All right. But just until then.

NARRATOR 1 And so life began for Hans Christian Andersen on April 2, 1805, in the little town of Odense (oh DENS) in the country of Denmark.

NARRATOR 2 Hans had a quiet childhood.

NARRATOR 3 But when he was seven, he was taken to the Odense Playhouse.

NARRATOR 4 The theater opened up a world full of wonder and magic for Hans.

HANS Words! Words of fancy, words of flight, words that fill me with delight!

MRS. ANDERSEN Keep still, little Hans, or these pins will stick you. *(Sighs.)* There now, I'm finished fitting your toga. Now you can play the part of Julius Caesar in style.

HANS Hurrah! I'm the greatest Caesar in all Odense!

DAGMAR I've no doubt, Hans. After all, Odense doesn't have many Caesars!

MRS. ANDERSEN *(laughs)* Well spoken, Dagmar!

2 Unit 2 • Work and Play

DAGMAR Well, I love Hans's little performances, Ma'am. Shall I go down to the cellar now to get the sheets from the hanging racks?

MRS. ANDERSEN Yes, dear. We still need to finish Mrs. Larsen's laundry.

SCENE 2

SOUND EFFECTS (*Knocking on door.*)

MRS. ANDERSEN I wonder who's at the door? Oh!

MR. NIELSEN Evening, Anne Marie.

MRS. ANDERSEN Good evening, Vilhelm. Gerta. Have you come to see Little Hans recite? As you can see, he's all dressed up in his toga. Hans—

HANS (*grandly*) "Cowards die many times before their deaths; the valiant never taste of death but once." That's from a play by William Shakespeare!

MRS. RASMUSSEN Another time, perhaps, dear little Hans.

MRS. ANDERSEN Then, what is it?

MR. NIELSEN Anne Marie, it's about your husband.

MRS. ANDERSEN Oh my! He's been captured, hasn't he?

MR. NIELSEN You see, Anne Marie—

MRS. ANDERSEN The day he signed up to be in Napoleon's army, I told him, "So your shop failed, and we're poor. That's no reason to play soldier!"

MRS. RASMUSSEN (*gently*) I'm afraid . . . Hans is dead, Anne Marie.

MRS. ANDERSEN (*after a long pause*) Put away your toga, Hans. There'll be no recital tonight.

HANS But Momma—

MRS. ANDERSEN (*sharply*) Put it away, I said! (*Sniffling.*) It's time you learned life isn't sunshine and roses, but misery and hard work!

The Boy Who Would Be Famous

MRS. RASMUSSEN Oh, Anne Marie—

MRS. ANDERSEN Gerta, do you still need an extra charwoman for your inn?

MRS. RASMUSSEN Yes, but—

MRS. ANDERSEN I'll be there, first thing in the morning. Now if you'll excuse me, I've some laundry to finish. Come along, Hans. Help me and Dagmar now.

SCENE 3

NARRATOR 1 Soon, life for the Andersens became harder and grimmer.

NARRATOR 2 With no money and little food, Hans's mother turned to her son.

MRS. ANDERSEN Get up, Hans! It's time you learned a trade.

HANS (sleepily) A trade, Momma?

MRS. ANDERSEN As an apprentice at the cloth mill—that means you'll be learning the job for a while before they hire you as a regular worker. You start today.

HANS But I'm only eleven.

MRS. ANDERSEN But you look fourteen. And anyway, you're a fast learner. You must help me put food on the table, or we shall starve.

NARRATOR 3 So Hans left for the cloth mill. But not long after he arrived—

SOUND EFFECTS (Polite clapping.)

HANS Thank you, and for my next song—

LARS No more songs, Screech Owl. I'm eating my lunch!

HANS Screech Owl?! But Lars, I thought—

SOREN Who says you can think, Hans? You're just an apprentice.

HANS Don't push me around, Soren! You're always treating the apprentices like dirt.

LARS That's because we came up the hard way. You'll do the same, Hans, if you know what's good for you.

HANS What a big lout you are, Lars. That's it! I quit.

SOREN You can't quit. You're an apprentice—you haven't learned the job yet!

NARRATOR 4 But Hans was as good as his word. He walked out and didn't look back. The only problem was, he still needed a job to help support his family.

NARRATOR 1 So the next week, Hans found work at a tobacco factory. But soon he developed a deep, burning cough and had to quit.

NARRATOR 2 At home once more and in poor health, he lost himself in books and daydreaming about the theater.

SCENE 4

NARRATOR 3 But then the Andersens' fortunes changed again.

DAGMAR Blessings, Mrs. Andersen, on this fine day! I wish you happiness!

MRS. ANDERSEN Thank you, dear Dagmar. Please join us for the wedding breakfast after the ceremony. Now that I'm to be the wife of a prosperous shoemaker, we'll have almond kringle and hot cocoa for breakfast every day!

NARRATOR 4 And so, Hans's mother married another shoemaker, but this time, a much more successful one. The Andersens now had plenty of food on their table, and Hans no longer had to work.

HANS Such nice clothes, Momma. Thank you! But what are they for?

MRS. ANDERSEN They're for the first day at your new school, Hans. Pastor Jensen has consented for you to start at the Odense Middle School today.

NARRATOR 1 Hans went to school, but he found the discipline strict and the subjects dull. Even worse, the teachers and students scorned his love of theater.

NIELS Look, Matilde. Here comes that odd boy, Hans Andersen.

The Boy Who Would Be Famous

MATILDE He's always reciting things, isn't he, Niels?

GUNNAR Yes, and it's too late to run away!

HANS Hello Gunnar, Niels. Greetings Matilde. Permit me to recite the words of Goethe (GEHR tuh), Germany's greatest writer: "Know you the land where the lemon-trees bloom? . . . There, there I would go, O my beloved, with thee!"

MATILDE Oh, that's beautiful, Hans!

NIELS Say, Hans, why can't you talk normal like the rest of us boys?

GUNNAR Perhaps he has crooked teeth—could that be reason, Niels?

NIELS AND GUNNAR (*laughing, ad lib*) Ha! Ha! That's rich. Ole' crooked tooth!

NARRATOR 2 At that, Hans squared his shoulders and stalked away.

GUNNAR Oh, he's a strange one, Niels.

NIELS Yes, he is. I wonder what will become of him.

NARRATOR 3 And at home, Momma was more impatient than ever with Hans.

MRS. ANDERSEN Hans, stop playing with those puppets! It's time you start learning a decent trade.

HANS (*sighs*) Which one?

MRS. ANDERSEN Anything! You're all but grown up. Do you want to find yourself living in a shack and wearing rags someday?

HANS I promise you, Momma, I will find a trade—as soon as school is out.

NARRATOR 4 At the end of the school year, Hans announced to Momma that he intended to seek his trade. He would go to Copenhagen and become an actor.

MRS. ANDERSEN (*shouting*) Have you gone mad?! What foolishness is this?

NARRATOR 1 And once again, they argued about Hans's lofty dreams.

SCENE 5

NARRATOR 2 Then, one day, something happened that gave Hans an idea.

MRS. ANDERSON Aaahh! Hans, say a prayer for me! I've just broken my mirror! Now, I fear, we will have seven years of hardship and suffering.

NARRATOR 3 For, you see, Mrs. Anderson was a very superstitious woman. Hans now knew how to get her blessing for his plans to go to Copenhagen.

NARRATOR 4 With the help of the ever-loyal Dagmar, Hans made a plan.

NARRATOR 1 Dagmar knew a fortuneteller named Madame Durga. That lady would visit Hans and his mother and play her part—as instructed by Dagmar.

MRS ANDERSEN Welcome, Madame Durga. Dagmar told me you'd be coming to our humble home. This is my son, Hans.

MADAME DURGA Mrs. Andersen! Hans! How kind of you to receive me.

MRS. ANDERSEN I've had a frightful experience, Madame. I just shattered my finest mirror, and I'm fearful about the future.

MADAME DURGA Mrs. Andersen, you need not be afraid. I see good health and prosperity in your future.

MRS ANDERSEN And for Hans, Madame Durga, what do you foresee for him?

MADAME DURGA Ah! Hans is destined for fame and fortune—but only if he goes to Copenhagen.

MRS. ANDERSEN Copenhagen? Hans, you were right. You must leave at once!

NARRATOR 2 And so, the arrangements were hastily made.

The Boy Who Would Be Famous

SCENE 6

NARRATOR 3 A few days later, Hans was waiting for the stagecoach to Copenhagen, his meager belongings bundled and strapped to his back.

HANS Dagmar! Say goodbye to me!

DAGMAR So our little plot worked! You are leaving for Copenhagen, then?

HANS Yes. Yes—thanks to you and Madame Durga.

DAGMAR Hans, stay safe in Copenhagen. And don't forget to write!

HANS Yes, I'll write, I promise. Goodbye, Dagmar.

NARRATOR 4 Just then, the stagecoach arrived, and Hans climbed in. As the coach bumped and creaked along, Hans gave his imagination free rein.

HANS (to himself) Aha! I have another idea for a story. How shall I begin it? Let's see . . . "There once was a baby duck who was so ugly that Momma Duck and the other ducklings would have nothing at all to do with him. . . ."

NARRATOR 1 Years later, when Hans Christian Andersen published his stories, "The Ugly Duckling" became a favorite of children everywhere. For the little boy from Odense grew up to be one of the world's greatest writers of fairy tales.

STORIES FOR A STARRY NIGHT
BY PETER GRAHAME

What do you see when you look up into the starry sky? You can make up your own story and share it.

CHARACTERS

CAMPERS 1–8
STAR TELLER
ORION
ARTEMIS
APOLLO
PARENT 1
PARENT 2
OLD MAN
SEVEN CHILDREN
THREE MONKEYS
BIG STAR
STAR 1
STAR 2
SKYGOD
TOUGH STAR
SEVEN LITTLE STARS

SCENE 1

CAMPER 1 This sure is a great campsite, isn't it?

CAMPER 2 Yeah, way out here in the wide open spaces.

CAMPER 3 It's so dark here—but at least we have a clear, starry sky tonight.

CAMPER 4 In fact, I've never seen such brightly burning stars!

CAMPER 5 I guess where we live, the bright lights on streets and in buildings keep the sky too lit up at night.

CAMPER 6 Hey! Look over there. You can see the Big Dipper.

CAMPERS *(ad lib)* Where? Huh? The what?

CAMPER 6 The Big Dipper. See? There are four bright stars that form the cup, and then those three stars there form the handle. It looks like a dipper, for drinking water.

CAMPER 7 Yes, and if you follow the first two stars in the cup, one above the other, they point right to . . .

CAMPER 8 I know! The North Star! There it is!

CAMPER 2 And the North Star is at the end of the handle of . . .

CAMPER 8 The Little Dipper!

CAMPER 1 I wonder who first thought they looked like dippers?

STAR TELLER Well, actually, some people think the Big Dipper looks like a bear.

CAMPERS *(ad lib)* What? Huh? Who said that?

CAMPER 1 Look! Right there! Sitting on that rock!

CAMPER 3 Excuse me. We didn't see you before. Where did you come from?

STAR TELLER Oh, here and there, up and down.

CAMPER 2 Who are you? Why is your robe shining like that?

STAR TELLER Well, you can call me Star Teller. And I'm here to talk about the stars, if you want to. It's my favorite subject.

CAMPERS *(ad lib)* Sure! Wow! You bet! Let's go!

SCENE 2

CAMPER 3 Star Teller, did you say the Big Dipper looks like a bear?

STAR TELLER Yes, to some people. You see, long ago, people looked up in the sky and saw patterns in the stars. You have a word that means "star pattern"—*constellation*. Did you know that? Well, to continue . . . people made up stories about constellations to explain how they came to be in the sky. Many Native Americans thought the first four stars of the Big Dipper could be a bear.

CAMPER 5 It doesn't look like a bear to me.

STAR TELLER Just use your imagination.

CAMPER 5 What about the three stars behind the bear?

CAMPER 6 I know! Bear hunters!

STAR TELLER That's right. Very good! And see that curve of stars over there?

CAMPER 7 Could that be the bear's cave?

STAR TELLER Right again! See? You understand. Let's take a look at another hunter. Look across the sky over there. See those three stars on an angle? That's known as the belt of Orion (uh REYE uhn) the hunter.

CAMPER 3 And those three smaller stars coming down from the belt, could that be his sword?

STAR TELLER Yes, that's right!

CAMPER 4 How did he get up there?

Stories for a Starry Night

STAR TELLER Well, there are many stories.

CAMPERS (ad lib) Tell us one, Star Teller. Yes! Tell us one!

STAR TELLER All right. Now listen carefully. Long ago, people in ancient Greece told of a hunter named Orion.

ORION That's me! I'm Orion. This stick is my sword!

STAR TELLER Okay, Orion. Tell us more about yourself.

ORION Yes, I will. I fell in love with Artemis (AR tuh muhs). She was a hunter too. A most beautiful hunter!

ARTEMIS Here I am, Orion. Here's your Artemis. Oh, how I love you!

STAR TELLER Unfortunately for Orion, Artemis was a goddess, goddess of the moon, in fact. It was her job to ride her chariot, the moon, across the sky each night. Now Artemis had a brother, Apollo. He was a powerful god, the sun god.

APOLLO I am the mighty Apollo! Sister . . . Artemis! You're supposed to be driving your moon chariot across the sky each night.

ARTEMIS Oh, Apollo. You're so stuck up! I'd rather be with Orion!

APOLLO Oh yeah? We'll see about that.

STAR TELLER It's a sad story. Apollo played a trick on his sister.

ARTEMIS Apollo! You made me shoot an arrow, and I hit Orion by mistake!

CAMPERS (ad lib) That's terrible! What happened then?

ARTEMIS I'll show you, Apollo! I'll take Orion and put him in the sky. Then, whenever I drive my moon chariot, I'll be up there with him!

CAMPERS (clapping, ad lib) Hooray! Good for her! A happy ending!

SCENE 3

CAMPER 4 Tell us another story, Star Teller!

STAR TELLER Very well. Look up above Orion's right shoulder. Do you see a small group of very dim stars?

CAMPER 2 I do! I think I can count . . . six!

STAR TELLER There are actually seven, but the last one is hard to see. That group of stars is known as the Pleiades (PLEE uh deez).

CAMPER 7 The . . . the . . . PLEE uh deez?

STAR TELLER That's right. And there are many stories from all over the world about how those seven stars came to be.

CAMPERS (ad lib) Tell us! Tell us a story! What are they?

STAR TELLER All right. Native Americans of many different tribes tell stories of how those seven stars came to be in the sky. One tribe, known as the Onondaga (OH nuhn DAY guh) tells this story. Once there were seven children . . .

SEVEN CHILDREN (together) We love to dance! We love to sing! We don't care about anything!

STAR TELLER Their parents were worried.

PARENT 1 Our children won't do their chores. They won't do their lessons.

PARENT 2 They won't even come home to eat! They just dance and sing all day and night. What are we to do?

STAR TELLER That night, an old man clothed in shining garments appeared to those dancing children.

OLD MAN Dancing and singing is all very good! But you children must stop now and go home to your parents. If you don't, something very strange will happen!

Stories for a Starry Night 5

SEVEN CHILDREN (*together*) You shine so bright, dear old man.
But we will dance as fast as we can!

STAR TELLER The seven children did get hungry, of course, so they ran home to their parents.

SEVEN CHILDREN (*together*) We want some food to take away.
So we can dance all night and day!

PARENT 1 If you want food, then you must come in and sit with us and eat!

PARENT 2 Now be good, like all the other children, and come inside!

STAR TELLER But the children wouldn't listen.

SEVEN CHILDREN (*together*) We've got to dance! We've got to sing!
So we won't eat, or anything! (*All laugh.*)

STAR TELLER That night, as they danced, the shining old man came once more.

OLD MAN I warn you! If you don't go home and be good to your parents, something very, very strange will happen to you!

STAR TELLER The children refused to listen—and then something strange did happen. Because they had not eaten, their bodies became very soft and light.

SEVEN CHILDREN (*together*) We're rising up! We're flying high!
We're going off into the sky! Help us! Help us! Me oh my!

STAR TELLER Their parents came running.

PARENT 1 Here's some food. Come back! Please come back!

PARENT 2 Please don't leave! Return to us!

STAR TELLER But the children could not come back. They had been turned into seven stars. We call them the Pleiades, but the Onondagas called them Oot-kwa-tah (oot KWAH tuh) and knew them to be seven children, forever dancing in a circle in the sky.

CAMPERS (*laughing, ad lib*) That was great! What a way to go! More. More!

SCENE 4

STAR TELLER Why don't you see what you can do with your own imaginations. Now if you look at the left end of Orion's belt and let your eyes continue on to the left, you'll see a very bright star called Sirius (SEER ee uhs). It is also known as the Dog Star.

CAMPER 6 Is it Orion's hunting dog?

STAR TELLER Could be.

CAMPER 7 Is there a story about that star too?

STAR TELLER Well, in India, they tell the story of a dog who followed his master to the Great Sky Land. But the gatekeeper there wouldn't let the dog in.

CAMPER 8 I'll bet the dog's owner loved the dog so much, he said he wouldn't go in without him. That's what I'd do.

STAR TELLER That's a good start. What happens next?

CAMPER 7 The dog wandered across the sky alone forever.

CAMPER 8 No, no, that's not right! The dog's owner wouldn't leave him alone like that.

CAMPER 3 I have a better idea! The gatekeeper was so impressed by the man's love for his dog, that he turned them both into beautiful stars of the night sky!

STAR TELLER Good, good! Now you're using your imaginations. You can look at a constellation and make up a story about it. People just like you have been doing that almost since the beginning of time.

CAMPER 5 But what if we get the wrong idea about a constellation? I mean what if we picture something really weird and different?

STAR TELLER My friend, there IS no right or wrong idea. In fact, there is a completely different story about the Pleiades, told by the Polynesian people of the Pacific Islands. They say that there was a Big Star that was very bright.

Stories for a Starry Night

BIG STAR That's me! Big Star! I am, in fact, the brightest star in the sky!

STAR TELLER He was also very, VERY vain.

BIG STAR Not only that, I am the brightest and most beautiful star in the sky.

STAR TELLER The other stars got rather tired of this.

STAR 1 I wish Big Star would be quiet already.

STAR 2 What a windbag!

STAR TELLER But the Big Star went on and on.

BIG STAR No, not just in the sky. I am the brightest and most beautiful star in the entire universe!

STAR 1 AND STAR 2 Skygod, Skygod, help us!

SKY GOD What? What is it? What do you want?

STAR 1 AND STAR 2 Please, please, Skygod, make Big Star stop bragging!

BIG STAR You can't stop me! I'm the best! Ha, ha!

SKY GOD Oh yes, I see. Well, we'll see about that. You there, Tough Star.

TOUGH STAR Who, me?

SKYGOD Yes, you. You're round and hard as a baseball. How about letting me practice my pitching?

TOUGH STAR Well, okay. I'd be glad to. But don't miss!

SKYGOD I won't.

STAR 1 *(like an announcer)* Skygod picks up Tough Star.

STAR 2 *(like an announcer)* Winding up for the pitch!

STAR 1 AND STAR 2 There it goes!

ALL AVAILABLE VOICES KA-BOOM! *(Ad lib.)* Yay! Hooray! He did it! Look at that!

STAR TELLER Yes, Big Star was shattered into seven smaller stars.

STAR 1 Well, that's the end of that.

STAR 2 There'll be no more bragging from now on.

STAR TELLER However, the Polynesian people say that if you listen very closely on a quiet night you can hear the voices of the seven little stars.

SEVEN LITTLE STARS (in tiny voices) We are the cutest and the prettiest and the brightest little stars in the entire universe! Hee, hee, hee!

STAR 1 AND STAR 2 Oh, no!

STAR TELLER And that's the end of the story!

CAMPER 2 Are there other stories about the Pleiades?

STAR TELLER Many. Native Americans told quite a few. Also people living long ago in Greece, Egypt, and India.

CAMPER 4 Oh Star Teller, tell us those stories now!

STAR TELLER No, I'm afraid my time is running out. But you can make up your own stories and share them. In fact, that's a lot more fun.

CAMPER 5 You mean, choose a star pattern in the sky . . .

CAMPER 6 And then make up a story about it?

STAR TELLER Other people did it. Why not you? Well, I have to go feed Sirius. 'Bye now. And good luck!

SCENE 5

CAMPER 7 Hey! Where did Star Teller go?

CAMPER 8 Vanished, it would seem.

CAMPER 1 Say, do you think Star Teller was serious?

CAMPER 6 No! Sirius was that dog.

CAMPER 1 No, no. I mean, was Star Teller *serious* about us making up our own star stories?

CAMPER 3 Why not? It kind of seemed like we were helping with the storytelling anyway.

CAMPER 4 Yeah! It was strange. Like in a dream or something.

CAMPER 5 Well, I want to try it. I pick those three stars in Orion's belt. I say they are . . . three monkeys in a row!

THREE MONKEYS *(together)* We see nothing, hear nothing, say nothing!

CAMPER 6 And so they got sent to the sky . . .

CAMPER 7 To learn something!

THREE MONKEYS *(together)* Now we know a lot—about the stars in the sky!

CAMPERS *(laughing, ad lib)* Yeah, that's it! That's the idea. This is great! Let's do more!

CAMPER 2 Okay. I'm going to make up my own constellation. See this bunch of people sitting around a campfire?

CAMPERS *(ad lib)* Huh? Who? Where?

CAMPER 2 Right here. All of us toasting marshmallows. And just maybe . . .

CAMPER 1 We'll turn into a constellation, too—the Marshmallow Toasters!

ALL CAMPERS *(together)* Here we go! Up to the sky!

The Twelve Dancing Princesses

Alisha Fran-Potter

based on a fairy tale from the Brothers Grimm

The king had a mystery, and he offered his kingdom to anyone clever enough to solve it.

CHARACTERS

KING
PRINCE ROMANO
MERVIN, a Baker
TONY, a Soldier
OLD WOMAN
TOWNSPERSON
PRINCESSES 1–12
NARRATORS 1–5

SCENE 1

NARRATOR 1 Once there was a King who was stumped by a great mystery.

NARRATOR 2 He had twelve daughters, the Princesses.

NARRATOR 3 They all slept together in a room with twelve beds in a row.

NARRATOR 4 Every night their father, the King, would kiss them goodnight and lock their bedroom door.

NARRATOR 5 In the morning when he came and unlocked the door, he found the Princesses' shoes placed in front of each of their beds.

NARRATOR 1 But the strange thing was that all those shoes were ruined, the soles worn right through.

KING I can't understand this. I myself lock their door each night. How could the Princesses get out? Where do they go?

NARRATOR 2 The King was happy enough to buy them new shoes every day, but the mystery about what they were doing was beginning to wear on his nerves.

NARRATOR 3 Finally, the King came up with a plan.

KING I declare a proclamation! Any man who can solve the mystery of the Princesses' shoes may choose one Princess to marry and inherit my kingdom.

TOWNSPERSON Does that mean that the man who inherits the kingdom will become king?

KING Well, um—yes. Someday. In the future. Eventually. Oh, but anyone who tries and fails will be banished from the kingdom.

TOWNSPERSON Well, good luck. But look, here comes someone now!

NARRATOR 4 And it must be said, the first man to present himself looked rather splendid.

SCENE 2

PRINCE ROMANO Your Majesty, I am Prince Romano. I wish to accept your challenge to solve the mystery of the Princesses' shoes.

KING Well, you're a very likely suitor. Very good, follow me.

NARRATOR 5 The King led Prince Romano to the Princesses' bedroom. Outside the door a chair had been placed so he could keep watch. This time the king didn't lock the door. Prince Romano took up his watch.

PRINCE ROMANO I'm bored, just sitting here waiting for something to happen. (Yawns.) I'll just close my eyes for a moment. (He snores.)

NARRATOR 1 And Prince Romano fell sound asleep. While the Princesses . . .

PRINCESS 1 Sister, go and check to see if Prince Romano is asleep.

PRINCESS 2 Why should I go? You go.

PRINCESS 3 Why don't you send the youngest?

PRINCESS 4 Well, someone go, or we won't have any time left.

PRINCESS 5 Let's have a contest to see who goes and checks on the Prince.

PRINCESS 6 No, that will take too long.

PRINCESS 7 We could draw feathers. The shortest has to go check.

PRINCESS 8 Just send someone. I'm busy finishing my hair.

PRINCESS 9 And I haven't yet chosen a dress for tonight.

PRINCESS 10 Me either. May I borrow your blue velvet gown?

PRINCESS 11 What about me? I need some jewelry to go with this.

PRINCESS 12 Stop! While you were arguing, I checked on Prince Romano. He's asleep. So let's go!

NARRATOR 2 The next morning, Prince Romano checked the Princesses' room. He saw all twelve asleep in their beds. He also saw twelve pairs of shoes worn completely through. Before long, the Prince was summoned before the King.

KING Well Prince Romano, did you solve the mystery? Do you know how my daughters manage to wear out their shoes each and every night?

PRINCE ROMANO I am sorry, Sire. Even though I stayed awake and vigilant all night, the shoes are still worn through. There's just no explanation.

KING Then what good are you? Go away! Never return to my kingdom again!

NARRATOR 3 So Prince Romano was banished from the kingdom. But that afternoon another man showed up at the palace.

SCENE 3

MERVIN I am Mervin the baker. I wish to accept your challenge to solve the mystery of the Princesses' shoes.

KING A baker, huh? Well, I did promise. Very good, follow me.

NARRATOR 4 The King showed Mervin the chair outside the Princesses' bedroom where he could keep watch.

MERVIN Well, this is going to be a piece of cake. But—oh!— I feel tired. I think I'll just close my eyes for a moment. *(He snores.)*

NARRATOR 5 And Mervin the baker fell sound asleep. While the Princesses . . .

PRINCESS 1 Sister, go and check to see if the baker is asleep.

PRINCESS 2 Why should I go? You go.

PRINCESS 3 Why don't you send the youngest?

PRINCESS 4 Well, someone go, or we won't have any time left.

PRINCESS 5 Let's have a contest to see who goes and checks on the baker.

PRINCESS 6 No, that will take too long.

PRINCESS 7 We could draw feathers. The shortest has to go check.

4 Unit 4 • *Puzzles and Mysteries*

PRINCESS 8 Just send someone. I haven't yet chosen a dress for tonight.

PRINCESS 9 Wait a minute, that's my line. You're supposed to be busy finishing your hair.

PRINCESS 10 Well, I need to borrow somebody's gown. Has anybody got a red satin in my size?

PRINCESS 11 What about me? I need some jewelry to go with this.

PRINCESS 12 Stop! While you were arguing, I checked on the baker. He's asleep. So let's go!

NARRATOR 1 The next morning, Mervin checked the Princesses' room. He saw all twelve asleep in their beds. He also saw twelve pairs of shoes worn completely through. Before long, Mervin was summoned before the King.

KING Well baker fellow—er—Mervin, did you solve the mystery? Do you know what my daughters do to their shoes?

MERVIN I am sorry, Sire. Even though I pinched myself to stay awake all night—see my arms?—the shoes are still worn through. There must be some kind of magic involved.

KING Magic, bah! Begone with you. Never return to my kingdom again!

NARRATOR 2 So Mervin the baker—like Prince Romano—was banished from the kingdom.

TOWNSPERSON It's too bad, really. A prince may not be worth much, but a good baker is hard to find!

SCENE 4

NARRATOR 3 News spread throughout the kingdom that two men had been banished for failing to solve the mystery of the Princesses' shoes.

NARRATOR 4 A soldier named Tony heard of the mystery.

TONY You know, I might just head over to the palace. I should have as good a chance as those other guys. And if I fail—well, I've always wanted to travel.

NARRATOR 5 Along the way Tony ran into an old woman.

OLD WOMAN And where might you be going, soldier?

TONY Well, Ma'am, I'm heading for the King's palace. I'm going to try and solve the mystery of the Princesses' shoes.

OLD WOMAN Some have tried and failed. But you might have a chance if you keep your wits about you. I have something here that will help you.

SOLDIER A cloak? What good will a cloak be to me?

OLD WOMAN Ah, my son. This is a magic cloak. When you put it on, it will make you invisible. You can follow the Princesses without being seen at all.

SOLDIER Thank you ever so much. But doesn't that sound kind of sneaky? Hey! Where did she go?

NARRATOR 1 For the old woman had disappeared into the shadows.

NARRATOR 2 The soldier put the cloak in his knapsack and continued on to the palace.

TONY Your Highness, I wish to accept your challenge to solve the mystery of the Princesses' shoes.

KING And who are you?

TONY Oh, I'm Tony. I'm a soldier, just retired from the army.

KING And now a soldier! Oh, very well, follow me.

NARRATOR 3 The King showed Tony the chair outside the Princesses' bedroom where he could keep watch.

TONY Now I wonder how long I have to wait. Well, while I'm waiting maybe I should try out this cloak the old woman gave me. Although it's hard to believe an invisible cloak . . .

NARRATOR 4 Meanwhile, the Princesses . . .

PRINCESS 1 Sister, go and check . . .

6 Unit 4 • *Puzzles and Mysteries*

PRINCESS 2 You go . . .

PRINCESS 3 Send the youngest . . .

PRINCESS 4 Well, someone go . . .

PRINCESS 5 Let's have a contest . . .

PRINCESS 6 Too long . . .

PRINCESS 7 Draw feathers . . .

PRINCESS 8 Just send someone . . .

PRINCESS 9 I haven't chosen . . .

PRINCESS 10 May I borrow that . . .

PRINCESS 11 What about me?

PRINCESS 12 Stop! While you were arguing, I went to check.

PRINCESS 2 Well?

PRINCESS 12 Well, sisters, Father must have come up empty-handed. There is no one at all watching us tonight!

ALL PRINCESSES *(ad lib)* Great! Hurry now! Let's party! Let's go!

SCENE 5

NARRATOR 5 The oldest Princess pressed a secret panel on her wardrobe. At once, a secret door opened wide, revealing a path winding through a beautiful forest.

NARRATOR 1 Meanwhile Tony—invisible, protected by the magic cloak—had seen the youngest Princess come out to check. Quietly, he followed her back in and was observing everything.

PRINCESS 3 Let's go, it's getting late.

PRINCESS 4 I have a strange feeling about tonight. Something isn't right.

PRINCESS 5 You're being silly. Come on!

The Twelve Dancing Princesses

PRINCESS 6 I'll take this candle, and you take that one. Let's go now.

TONY (to himself) This really is a magic cloak the old woman gave me! I can follow the Princesses, and they don't see a thing.

NARRATOR 2 Just at that moment, Tony accidentally stepped on one of the Princesses' dresses.

PRINCESS 7 Who's tugging on my dress?

PRINCESS 8 Oh, it's just caught on something. Here, let me free it up.

NARRATOR 3 The Princesses—and Tony—followed the path into the forest.

NARRATOR 4 It was beautiful and quite magical.

NARRATOR 5 Jewels hung from branches, and gold dust sparkled on the trees.

NARRATOR 1 All the while, Tony was thinking about his mission.

TONY I'd better take some proof to show the King. I'll snap a branch off one of these trees. Oh good! When I hold it in my hand, it becomes invisible too.

PRINCESS 9 Hey, did you hear THAT? Could someone be following us?

PRINCESS 10 I think not. Perhaps our hosts are firing a gun salute to welcome us.

NARRATOR 2 For the Princesses were, in fact, on their way to a great castle.

NARRATOR 3 Suddenly, it loomed into view, shining and magnificent.

TONY (gasping loudly) Wow!

PRINCESS 11 Which one of you said that?! Did someone see a wild beast?

PRINCESS 12 Oh, it's nothing, to be sure. Hurry! We'll be late.

NARRATOR 4 The twelve Princesses entered the castle and made their way quickly to the ballroom.

NARRATOR 5 Where they met their escorts and danced the night away.

NARRATOR 1 Tony watched every tap of the foot, every dip and twirl. Though in the midst of the ball, he remained quite invisible.

TONY I'd better take some more proof to show the King. I'll take this wine goblet. No one will miss it.

NARRATOR 2 Just before the first light of dawn, the Princesses returned on the forest path and passed through the secret door.

NARRATOR 3 Tony made sure he got through the door too, before it closed up again.

NARRATOR 4 Each Princess went to her bed, laid her shoes on the floor, and crawled into the covers.

NARRATOR 5 But Tony made his way to the King's audience room.

SCENE 6

KING Well, soldier?

TONY Call me Tony, Sire.

KING Uh—Tony, do you know where my daughters are going and why their shoes are worn out every morning?

SOLDIER Your daughters have been wearing out their shoes while dancing with princes at a ball in a gleaming castle at the edge of an enchanted forest. Here is proof. From the enchanted forest, I bring you this gold-dusted tree branch. From the castle ballroom, I bring you this wine goblet.

KING Goodness me! So it was magic, after all! Summon my daughters!

PRINCESS 2 Did you call for us, Daddy?

KING Girls, Is it true what this soldier tells me about a castle ballroom in an enchanted forest?

PRINCESS 6 Uh-oh. We've been outsmarted!

PRINCESS 3 But where did he come from? I could have sworn there was no one . . .

PRINCESS 4 I told you I had a strange feeling!

PRINCESS 5 Oh, you're always having strange feelings!

KING Well, Girls?

PRINCESS 2 Yes, Father, it is true.

KING My dear boy, you've solved the mystery. When I am gone, you'll become king. For now, you may choose one of my daughters to wed.

SOLDIER Sire, I'll take the eldest. I think she has spirit.

PRINCESS 1 *(to the other Princesses)* Good! I like him quite well.

NARRATOR 1 The wedding was held the next day. It was a grand day, filled with delicious food, fabulous costumes, music, and—of course—dancing, dancing, dancing!

TOWNSPERSON What a party! And just think—there are eleven more Princesses. That means eleven more royal weddings and eleven more parties!

To Go with the FLOW

by Susan DiLallo

Reluctant to say goodbye to her old life, a young girl discovers the adventure of a lifetime on a flatboat journey down the Ohio and Mississippi Rivers in the 1830s.

CHARACTERS

MARTHA HUTCHINS (9 years)
AARON HUTCHINS (6 years)
MRS. HUTCHINS
MR. HUTCHINS
UNCLE ENOCH
ZEKE, the Carpenter
ELLA MAY (10 years)
SARAH (9 years)
NED, the Navigator
NARRATORS 1–6
SOUND EFFECTS

SCENE 1

NARRATOR 1 The place: Louisville, Kentucky. The time: 1830. The Hutchins family—Mother, Father, Martha, and little Aaron—are about to leave behind their home and friends in Kentucky and move to Louisiana.

MARTHA But Mother, why can't we stay here? Why do we have to move?

MRS. HUTCHINS Martha, you know what a hard time we've had on the farm this year. What we need is good land and ample rain. Your Uncle Enoch (EE nuck) says . . .

MARTHA I know, I've read his letters. He always says the same thing . . .

UNCLE ENOCH *(as he writes)* Come down here, Brother. The land's fertile, and there are good farms for sale. We could be a family again.

MARTHA But all my friends are HERE, Mother. Especially Ella May and Sarah.

MRS. HUTCHINS You'll make new friends, Martha. Uncle Enoch says . . .

MARTHA Uncle Enoch again! I'm so tired of Uncle Enoch. He's ruining my life!

MRS. HUTCHINS That's an awful thing to say, Martha. Every time he writes, he says loving things about you . . .

UNCLE ENOCH How is your precious Martha? I remember what a little angel she was the last time I saw her . . . so many years ago.

MARTHA I don't care. I hate him!

MR. HUTCHINS That's QUITE enough, young lady! Now help your mother, quietly.

SCENE 2

NARRATOR 2 The next day, Father hired Zeke, the carpenter, to build the flatboat that would take the family down the Ohio River and then the Mississippi River to their new farm near New Orleans.

ZEKE Mr. Hutchins, I've pounded together many a flatboat. I can build a good one for you . . . with help from you and a few other good hands.

NARRATOR 3 The next day, Zeke, Father, and several neighbors began work on the boat's wooden frame. They worked hard through one day, then another.

SOUND EFFECTS (Hammering.)

ZEKE Good job! Now we'll fasten these green oak planks to the frame.

SOUND EFFECTS (Hammering continues under.)

NARRATOR 4 With each beat of the hammer, all Martha could think of was . . .

MARTHA (in rhythm with the hammering) No! No! No! No! No! No!

NARRATOR 5 But the hammering went on.

ZEKE Now we'll caulk the sides with pitch—to keep the water out.

NARRATOR 6 Then, to each end they fastened long wooden oars to steer with.

ZEKE Good work, everyone. She's finished now!

SCENE 3

NARRATOR 1 Father and Mother took Martha and Aaron to see their new floating home.

AARON Wow! Look at that . . . er . . .

MR. HUTCHINS Flatboat, son. It's called that because the bottom is flat.

MARTHA It looks like a big square wooden box instead of a boat.

MR. HUTCHINS Well, it floats. It will get us to Louisiana. Step aboard.

MRS. HUTCHINS See, in the rear, children? There's a chimney so we can cook our meals.

AARON What's that shed in the middle, Momma?

MRS. HUTCHINS That's the cabin, Aaron. We'll sleep and stay out of bad weather there.

MARTHA What are those little rooms in the back for, Father?

MR. HUTCHINS That's where we'll keep the horses, cows, and chickens.

MARTHA Father, how long will it take us to get to Louisiana?

MR. HUTCHINS About four weeks, Martha.

MARTHA Four awful weeks of stinky animals. They're supposed to live in barns!

MR. HUTCHINS You'll feel better, Martha, once we get started early tomorrow morning.

SCENE 4

NARRATOR 2 But Martha felt much worse the next morning because she had to say goodbye to the friends she'd known all her life—Ella May and Sarah.

ELLA MAY You'll write to us, won't you, Martha? And tell us about your new life?

MARTHA Of course, Ella May.

SARAH We'll miss you. It just won't be the same without you.

MARTHA I know, Sarah. I feel the same way. *(Sniffles, trying to hold back tears.)*

ELLA MAY Here, Martha. I want you to have this.

MARTHA Your velvet shawl? Oh, Ella May, I couldn't take it. You love it so.

ELLA MAY Nonsense. You're my best friend. Think of me when you wear it.

SARAH And here's something from me, Martha—my lucky silver dollar.

MARTHA Oh, thank you, Sarah, thank you both!

NARRATOR 3 Martha hugged her friends good-bye a final time.

SCENE 5

NARRATOR 4 Now everything was loaded on the flatboat. The animals too.

SOUND EFFECTS (chickens clucking) Cluck, cluck, cluck . . . .

SOUND EFFECTS (cows mooing) Mooooo . . . Mooooo . . . .

SOUND EFFECTS (horses neighing) Neighhhh . . . Neighhhh . . . .

MR. HUTCHINS Children, this is Ned. He'll be our navigator on the river.

NED Hey, young'uns. All aboard!

NARRATOR 5 Ned untied the boat from the dock. Soon it was drifting downriver with the current. For hours, Martha listened to water slapping at the boat's side.

MARTHA (to herself) This is so boring! Will every day be like this?

MR. HUTCHINS I'm going to light the fire now. Martha and Aaron, help your Mother get the stew ready for dinner.

NARRATOR 6 As night fell, Ned aimed the boat for shore and grabbed hold of some branches.

AARON Why are you doing that, Ned?

NED We use the branches like handles to pull us toward land, Aaron. That way, we can ground the boat and anchor it for the night, so it doesn't drift.

NARRATOR 1 Day Two was much like Day One. On Day Three, they passed some other flatboats tied together.

AARON Ned, why are those boats tied like that?

NED Well, Aaron, some people think it protects them against river pirates.

MARTHA Pirates? Could this trip get any worse? I wish I were still back home!

SCENE 6

NARRATOR 2 But the trip went smoothly enough. Until Day Seven, when suddenly . . .

SOUND EFFECTS *(big crash)* CRUNCH . . . !!!!

NARRATOR 3 The boat lurched forward. Father, who'd been standing on the deck, was thrown to the side, and hit his head. It began to bleed badly.

MRS. HUTCHINS Children! Your father's been hurt! He's bleeding. Aaron, take off your shirt and tear it up the back. I'll need to make a bandage to stop the blood.

AARON Yes, Momma.

NARRATOR 4 Just then, Martha came out of the cabin. But before she could help Mrs. Hutchins with the bandaging . . .

NED Martha! Come here, fast! I need you to help me row.

MARTHA Me? I don't know anything about rowing!

NED Not a lot to know. Hurry! Grab onto that pole and lean into it. Attagirl! Slow, like this. Good. Now, ease it way back—and again. See? We're turning.

MARTHA What happened back there?

NED I think we hit a wooden island.

MARTHA A what?

NED A wooden island. That's what they call floating logs. Now, if we can just get past this log jam, everything will be okay and . . .

SOUND EFFECTS *(big crash)* CRACK!

MARTHA Now what?

NARRATOR 5 Ned pointed to a spot near the front of the boat where a piece of log had broken through. It was a small hole, but water began spurting in.

6 Unit 5 • **Adventures by Land, Air, and Water**

NED I'd say we snagged a planter—that's a log that's lodged on the river bottom and sticks way up in the current. . . . It's a hole, all right. A hole clear through.

AARON What's gonna happen to us? I can't swim very far. Momma, I'm scared!

NED I know something we can try. A boat captain downriver once told me that he plugged a hole like this with a blanket. He threw it overboard, then the suction of the water rushing into the hole pulled the blanket in . . . and stopped the leak! Quick! We need to find a blanket or a good, heavy cloth!

MARTHA Here, Ned. Maybe you can plug it up with . . . this.

MRS. HUTCHINS Oh, Martha—not your shawl! Why, Ella May gave that to you.

MARTHA We can't think about that now, Mother. Take it, Ned.

NED Okay. That shawl looks about right, Martha—thick and heavy. The hole is just below water level. I'll put the shawl against it on the outside—like this.

MARTHA Will it work, Ned?

NED Yes! It's getting sucked into the hole, like they said. It will hold for now, and I can make a better patch later. Your quick thinking saved the day, Martha!

SCENE 7

NARRATOR 6 Meanwhile, Father was coming to.

MR. HUTCHINS Oh . . . what happened?

MRS. HUTCHINS We hit some logs. You hurt your head. How do you feel?

MR. HUTCHINS A little dizzy, but . . . okay. The children . . . ?

MRS. HUTCHINS They're fine.

To Go with the Flow

NED Oh, they're more than fine! Your daughter here is just about the bravest kid I ever met. Why, if it wasn't for her cool head, there's no telling where we'd be.

NARRATOR 1 Ned explained to Mr. Hutchins exactly what had happened.

NED We've got an old family tradition, Sir. We name the boat after the most important person on board.

NARRATOR 2 With that, Ned pulled a piece of chalk out of his pocket, walked to the front wall of the cabin, and wrote in big block letters—

MARTHA "The Intrepid Martha"!

AARON What does *intrepid* mean, Ned?

NED It means "bold; fearless," Aaron.

AARON That's you, Martha!

MR. HUTCHINS Daughter, how does it feel to be the hero of the hour?

MARTHA A hero? Gee. I never thought of myself as that before.

MR. HUTCHINS You never know what you're capable of doing . . . until you have to do it.

NARRATOR 3 That night, Martha's clothes still felt dirty and itchy, and the animals still smelled bad. But Martha couldn't help smiling about the day's events.

NARRATOR 4 She had lost a prized possession—Ella May's shawl—but after all, she had used it to save the boat and her family.

MARTHA *(to herself)* Ella May will understand. And I still have Sarah's silver dollar.

MR. AND MRS. HUTCHINS Good night now, children.

MARTHA AND AARON Good night, Mother and Father.

MARTHA Mother? Father? I can hardly wait to tell Uncle Enoch about what happened today!

Carla's Race

by Amy Fellner Dominy

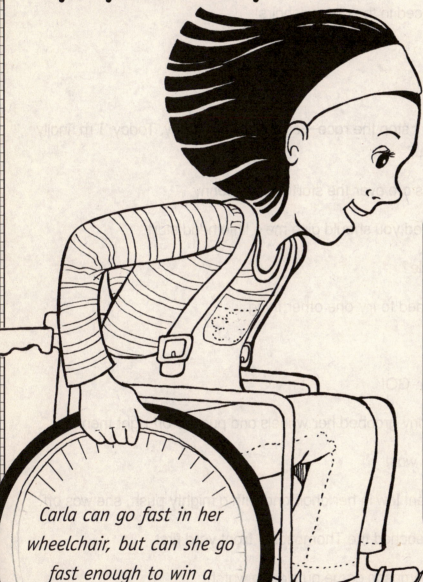

Carla can go fast in her wheelchair, but can she go fast enough to win a wheelchair race?

CHARACTERS

CARLA WALTERS (10 years)
JENNY (9 years)
MRS. WALTERS
MR. WALTERS
JIMMY WALTERS (13 years)
COLLEEN WALTERS (15 years)

MRS. THOMPSON
MR. WEAVER
OFFICIAL
CONCESSIONS LADY
NATALIE FLORES (10 years)

NARRATORS 1–6

SCENE 1

NARRATOR 1 Every Friday after school, Jenny and Carla had a race.

JENNY All right, Carla. On your mark.

NARRATOR 2 They raced down Carla's street—from the end of the cul de sac (KUHL duh sak) to Carla's driveway.

JENNY Get set.

NARRATOR 3 They raced in their wheelchairs!

JENNY Go!

CARLA Wait!

JENNY Carla, you can't stop the race—especially not today. Today, I'm finally going to beat you!

CARLA But your wheels are over the starting line, Jenny.

JENNY I know. I decided you should give me a little head start.

CARLA You call that little?

JENNY Oh, and I decided to try one other thing.

CARLA What's that?

JENNY A surprise start. GO!

NARRATOR 4 And Jenny grabbed her wheels and pushed off right then.

CARLA (laughing) Hey, wait!

NARRATOR 5 Carla bent low in her chair and with a mighty push, she was off.

NARRATOR 6 Jenny reached the Thompsons' front yard first.

NARRATOR 1 Mrs. Thompson came outside to watch.

MRS. THOMPSON You're doing great, Girls!

CARLA Thanks, Mrs. Thompson.

NARRATOR 2 Carla spun her arms around the wheels even faster.

NARRATOR 3 The wind blew her hair around her face.

NARRATOR 4 Dust flew up from her tires.

JENNY (calling out) I'm at the Weavers' house!

NARRATOR 5 Mr. Weaver stood outside trimming bushes.

MR. WEAVER It looks like a new world record!

NARRATOR 6 Another minute, and Jenny would be at Carla's driveway.

NARRATOR 1 Carla's mom, Mrs. Walters, her brother Jimmy, and her sister Colleen all came out to watch and cheer.

MRS. WALTERS Way to go, girls!

JIMMY Come on, Carla, you can do it!

COLLEEN You're almost home!

CARLA (calling out) I'm going to catch you, Jenny!

JENNY (panting) Not . . . today!

NARRATOR 2 Then, with a burst of speed, Carla zoomed past Jenny and crossed the finish line first.

JENNY (breathless) I . . . can't believe . . . you beat me . . . again!

CARLA Just by a little.

MRS. WALTERS That was a close finish.

CARLA Thanks, Mom.

SCENE 2

JENNY You know, Carla, my dad showed me a brochure about a wheelchair race at the high school next month. Kids come from all over to compete. I haven't had my birthday yet so I'm not old enough. But you could enter.

MRS. WALTERS That's a great idea, Jenny.

CARLA But I've never been in a real race.

JENNY It's a 400-meter race—that's one time around the school track.

CARLA I've never raced that far.

JIMMY I could help you train, Carla. When my track team practices, we do sprints around the track, rest, then sprint again. You could do the same thing in your wheelchair.

CARLA Jimmy, I'd be too nervous to enter a real race.

COLLEEN I get nervous before swim meets. I can help you with that, Carla.

JENNY And I'll be your cheerleader . . . *(Cheering.)*
Carla, Carla you can race,
You're the one who sets the pace!

CARLA *(laughing)* All right, you guys—you win.

JIMMY No, Carla—YOU'RE going to win!

NARRATOR 3 The next day, Carla filled out the entry form with her dad.

NARRATOR 4 And then the training began.

SCENE 3

MR. WALTERS Instead of grabbing the rims of your wheels, Carla, hit the rims to push yourself forward. You'll go faster.

CARLA I'll try, Dad. But what if I'm not as good as the other kids?

COLLEEN Don't think about the other kids.

CARLA How do I stop thinking about them, Colleen? They'll be all around me.

COLLEEN Just focus on doing the best race you can do.

NARRATOR 5 Jimmy timed her racing around the track.

JIMMY That was your fastest time yet, Carla. Rest a couple of minutes, and we'll do it again.

CARLA (breathless) Again? I can't do it again. I'm tired!

JIMMY That's good. That means you're getting stronger.

NARRATOR 6 And Jenny cheered her on.

JENNY (cheering)
Carla, Carla she's a blast,
In her chair she's really fast!

NARRATOR 1 Finally, it was the day of the big race.

MR. WALTERS Don't worry, Carla. It's okay to be a little nervous.

CARLA Is it okay to be really, REALLY nervous, Dad?

MR. WALTERS You'll be fine. It'll be just like racing Jenny down our street.

SCENE 4

NARRATOR 2 But when they arrived at the high school, it was nothing like Terrace Street.

NARRATOR 3 The track was a whirlwind of activity and noise.

NARRATOR 4 Officials had set up a podium with a microphone.

OFFICIAL (calling out) Testing. Testing.

NARRATOR 5 A lady called from a concession booth.

CONCESSIONS LADY Lemonade, ice cold lemonade!

NARRATOR 6 The bleachers around the track were filled with noisy spectators.

NARRATOR 1 And on the track, girls in wheelchairs warmed up.

JENNY Carla, see the girl dressed all in purple?

CARLA Wow, she's fast!

JENNY That's Natalie Flores.

CARLA Do you know her, Jenny?

JENNY I've heard of her. She wins a lot of races.

CARLA I can see why!

MR. WALTERS Carla, come on. It's time to warm up your arms.

JENNY Good luck!

CARLA Thanks, Jenny. I'll need it!

SCENE 5

NARRATOR 2 The Official's voice boomed through the microphone.

OFFICIAL (calling out) Racers, to your lanes.

MR. WALTERS Okay, Carla, this is it.

CARLA I feel like I'm going to be sick.

COLLEEN Good. That's just how I feel before I have my best races.

MRS. WALTERS You'll be fine, Carla, just like at home.

CARLA I wish this really were Terrace Street!

NARRATOR 3 Slowly, Carla rolled into her spot at the start of Lane Three. Next to her, the girl in purple waited.

CARLA Hi. I'm Carla Walters.

NATALIE Hi, Carla. I'm Natalie Flores.

CARLA Hi, Natalie.

NATALIE Well, good luck Carla!

CARLA Thanks . . . and good luck to you too!

OFFICIAL (*calling out*) Racers, take your marks.

CARLA (*to herself, nervously*) I don't know if I can do this!

OFFICIAL (*calling out*) Get set.

NARRATOR 4 Just then, Carla heard another voice.

JENNY (*cheering*)
    Carla, Carla do not fuss,
    Make those kids all eat the dust!

OFFICIAL (*calling out*) GO!

NARRATOR 5 Just like at home, Carla reacted to the command.

NARRATOR 6 She bent low, lifted her arms, and pushed off.

NARRATOR 1 She caught a glimpse of someone waving from the stands.

MRS. THOMPSON Go, Carla! You're looking great.

CARLA (*calling out*) Thanks, Mrs. Thompson!

NARRATOR 2 Her arms flew around the wheels, hitting the rim at the top just like her dad taught her.

NARRATOR 3 Wind whistled through her hair.

NARRATOR 4 Dust flew up from her wheels.

NARRATOR 5 In her mind, she pictured the Weaver's house coming up next.

MR. WEAVER (*calling out*) It's a world-record day, Carla!

NARRATOR 6 Faster and faster, she propelled the wheels of her chair, whipping around the curve.

CARLA (*breathless*) There's the finish line—I can make it!

NARRATOR 1 She gave a last burst of effort—

NARRATOR 2 And flew over the finish line!

NARRATOR 3 A moment later, she was surrounded by family and friends.

ALL AVAILABLE VOICES (cheering, ad lib) Way to go! Champion! Good race!

OFFICIAL (calling out) Ladies and Gentleman, the winner is—Carla Walters!

JENNY Did you hear that, Carla? You won!

CARLA (surprised) I won?

JIMMY You didn't know?

CARLA At first I was really nervous, but then I forgot all about the race. Jenny's cheer made me laugh. Then I heard the neighbors cheering. It didn't seem so scary anymore. I just imagined I was racing down Terrace Street!

Poetry Interpretation

To **interpret** poetry means to read it aloud for an audience. You use your *voice,* your *body,* and your *facial expressions* to get the meaning of the poetry across.

Some poems tell stories. They name characters and describe the actions of the characters as they go to school, get in trouble, go on adventures, and so on. With poems like these, you need to figure out who the characters are. Characters may be people, animals, or even inanimate objects, like rocks or tools. You also need to figure out what the relationship is between the characters. Is there a conflict? That's important to understand.

Some storytelling poems have speeches, like dialogue in a play. A poem with dialogue may be just one long speech by one character. Then you can act that character's part when you interpret the poem.

A poem with dialogue may have speeches by two or more characters talking back and forth. Then you can read it with some friends, each of you acting one character's part. Or, you can act all the characters yourself. You can use different character voices and different facial expressions.

Other poems do not tell stories. They may simply describe interesting scenes or tell about how the speaker feels. Sometimes a reader can't be sure who the speaker is supposed to be. Then you might imagine yourself as the speaker. Imagine yourself feeling the way the speaker feels and using words the speaker uses.

WHAT DOES IT MEAN?

When you interpret poetry, your first job is to make the audience understand what is going on. To do that, you have to be sure you understand it yourself. Here are some pointers:

- *Understand every word.* Use a dictionary for any word you're not sure of. Remember that many words have more than one meaning. Also be sure you understand any references to fairy tales, myths, history, and so on.

- *Think about the title.* What does it tell you about the poem? Does it suggest new meanings for the poem?

- *Look for the meaning.* Look for complete sentences. Use punctuation to help you know when to pause. Some poems are not written in sentences. In that case, look for complete thoughts. Think about how you can use your voice to get those thoughts across.

WHAT SHOULD IT SOUND LIKE?

After you understand the poem, you have to get your understanding across to your audience. Ask yourself these questions:

- *What is the style or mood of the poem?* Is it funny or serious? Is it full of surprise or full of anger? Is it written in simple, everyday language or in a more formal language?

- *What is the rhythm of the poem?* Does it call for a quick, light reading or a slow, thoughtful one? Be sure you stress the syllables in words that are stressed naturally in speech.

- *Does it rhyme?* The rhymes of a poem can create great fun. But as an interpreter, usually you do not need to stress the rhymes. If you read to get across the meaning, the rhymes should simply fall into place.

- *How about emphasis?* Some poems seem to call for a fairly even pace and emphasis throughout, like a walk through a park. Others may call for changes in volume or strength to stress words, ideas, or images, like a game of tag. You can use loudness to emphasize words. You can use a strong voice to emphasize words. You can even use silence. If you pause before or after a word, that can emphasize it too.

- *How can you phrase to express the meaning of the poem?* To **phrase** means to group words together. You should group words together so they are easier to understand. You *don't* have to pause at the end of each line. In fact, it may destroy the meaning if you try to do so. Experiment with different phrasings. Read for the punctuation, if that is helpful. Otherwise, read for the ideas.

YOUR PERFORMANCE

Think about things good storytellers do to hold their audiences' attention. You can do those things when you interpret poetry.

Practice your interpretation aloud several times before you perform it. If possible, practice in front of a mirror. You might also ask a classmate or family member to give you helpful feedback.

Be sure you know how to pronounce every word. Use a dictionary for any word you're not sure of. Practice the difficult words and difficult word combinations until you can say them smoothly without stumbling.

Take your time. When you step in front of your audience, don't rush into your performance. Take a few deep breaths and focus on the job you are doing. At the end, pause, look at your audience, and smile, to let them know your performance is finished.

Make eye contact with your audience. You don't have to memorize the poem you are reading. You should be familiar enough with it, though, that you can look up from your paper from time to time.

Be sure to speak loudly enough. You need to be heard all around the room—including the back row.

Choral Speaking

The word **choral** usually refers to a choir or chorus. In choral speaking, it means a small group or a whole class reading together. Sometimes the readers take turns, and sometimes they speak all together. This can be an exciting way to explore a poem with a wide variety of voices.

THE SCRIPT

First you need to decide who reads what lines. Decide how many solo voices you will use and how you are going to group the other voices (all boys, all girls, chorus 1, chorus 2, and so on). Then divide the lines among the available voices. Remember that a single voice or a combination of voices or the whole group might read a single line—or a single word. Once lines have been assigned, a director or a group of two or three readers can write the script.

Use your imagination here. You know voices can sing or hum; they can sound happy or sad; they can sound like animals or machines or like wind through the trees. Think about what special sound effects would work for your poem. Then think about how to create those sounds with your voices.

REHEARSAL AND PERFORMANCE

To give a good choral performance you must rehearse. If possible, have a director who signals individuals and groups when to come in. If there is no director, assign one strong reader to start off each choral section so that the rest of the group can come in immediately. You want to give the impression that all voices start and stop together.

Plan your entrances and exits. Also plan where all the people stand or sit when they are not reading. Remember, even when you are not the one reading, you are still onstage. You must do your part to direct the audience's attention by keeping your focus on the ones who are reading.

Poetry Interpretation

Unit 1 This Land Is Your Land

Idaho

by Kaye Starbird

Farmers out in Idaho
Plant potatoes, row on row.
Then before the green vines show
Every farmer has to go
Daily hoe-ing with his hoe
Up and down the rows till—lo—
Finally potatoes grow.

This, potato farmers know:
What comes up must start below;
What you reap you have to sow;
What you grow you have to hoe.

If you don't like farming, though,
    And you've never *tried* a hoe
    Or you hate to guide a hoe
    Or you can't abide a hoe
Stay away from Idaho.

---

lo Look! See!

Unit 2 Work and Play

The Swing
by Robert Louis Stevenson

How do you like to go up in a swing,
    Up in the air so blue?
Oh, I do think it the pleasantest thing
    Ever a child can do!

Up in the air and over the wall,
    Till I can see so wide,
Rivers and trees and cattle and all
    Over the countryside—

Till I look down on the garden green;
    Down on the roof so brown—
Up in the air I go flying again,
    Up in the air and down!

Monday!
by David L. Harrison

Overslept
Rain is pouring
Missed the bus
Dad is roaring
Late for school
Forgot my spelling
Soaking wet
Clothes are smelling
Dropped my books
Got them muddy
Flunked a test
Didn't study
Teacher says
I must do better
Lost my money
Tore my sweater
Feeling dumber
Feeling glummer
Monday sure can be
A bummer.

Unit 3 Patterns in Nature

The Seed

by Aileen Fisher

How does it know,
this little seed,
if it is to grow
to a flower or weed,
if it is to be
a vine or shoot,
or grow into a tree
with a long deep root?
A seed is so small
where do you suppose
it stores up all
of the things it knows?

A Young Farmer of Leeds

Anonymous

There was a young farmer of Leeds
Who swallowed six packets of seeds.
    It soon came to pass
    He was covered with grass,
And couldn't sit down for the weeds.

Unit 3 Patterns in Nature

Rain in Summer
by Henry Wadsworth Longfellow

How beautiful is the rain!
After the dust and heat,
In the broad and ferry street,
In the narrow lane,
How beautiful is the rain!
How it clatters along the roofs,
Like the tramp of hoofs!

How it gushes and struggles out
From the throat of the overflowing spout!
Across the window pane
It pours and pours;
And swift and wide,
With a muddy tide,
Like a river down the gutter roars
The rain, the welcome rain!

---

broad and ferry street A broad street is a wide main street. A ferry street is one heading to a river where a ferry boat is docked.

Unit 4 Puzzles and Mysteries

The Mysterious Smirkle

by Brian Patten

Some say the Smirkle was a Smatterbug
And loved to smatterbug about,
But exactly what it was or did
We never did find out.

Was the Smirkle friendly?
Was it calm, meek and mild?
Or was it mean and nasty,
Belligerent and wild?

Did it live on cabbages,
Or did it live on Mars?
Was it made of chocolate drops,
Or formed by the light of stars?

It's one of Life's small mysteries
And gladly goes to show
There are still things left on the earth
That we will never know.

Unit 4 Puzzles and Mysteries

Have You Ever Seen?

Anonymous

Have you ever seen a sheet on a river bed?
Or a single hair from a hammer's head?
Has the foot of a mountain any toes?
And is there a pair of garden hose?

Does the needle ever wink its eye?
Why doesn't the wing of a building fly?
Can you tickle the ribs of a parasol?
Or open the trunk of a tree at all?

Are the teeth of a rake ever going to bite?
Have the hands of a clock any left or right?
Can the garden plot be deep and dark?
And what is the sound of the birch's bark?

Unit 5 Adventures by Land, Air, and Water

Sea Fever

by John Masefield

I must go down to the seas again,
   to the lonely sea and the sky,
And all I ask is a tall ship
   and a star to steer her by;
And the wheel's kick and the wind's song
   and the white sail's shaking,
And the gray mist on the sea's face,
   and a gray dawn breaking.

I must go down to the seas again,
   for the call of the running tide
Is a wild call and a clear call
   that may not be denied;
And all I ask is a windy day
   with the white clouds flying,
And the flung spray and the blown spume,
   and the seagulls crying.

I must go down to the seas again,
   to the vagrant gypsy life,
To the gull's way and the whale's way
   where the wind's like a whetted knife,
And all I ask is a merry yarn
   from a laughing fellow-rover,
And a quiet sleep and a sweet dream
   when the long trick's over.

---

spume foam or froth caused by the sea's waves
vagrant wandering

Unit 5 Adventures by Land, Air, and Water

Moonwalker

by Carol Diggery Shields

I'm a moonwalker, walking on the moon.
I'm a jungle stalker, stalking wild baboons.
I'm a superhero, skimming through the blue.
Puddle jumping, leaf-pile leaping, I'm a kangaroo.

I'm a desert rattlesnake, sliding through the sand.
Counting out the beat, I'm the leader of the band.
I'm Tyrannosaurus, looking for a snack.
Whoo-whoo! I'm a train, rolling down the track.

I'm a red-eyed robot, clanking up the road.
I'm an eighteen-wheeler with a heavy load.
I'm a famous rock star, moving very cool.
Actually,
    I'm just me,
        Walking home from school.

Unit 6 Reaching for Goals

To Dark Eyes Dreaming
by Zilpha Keatley Snyder

Dreams go fast and far
   these days.
They go by rocket thrust.
They go arrayed
   in lights
      or in the dust of stars.
Dreams, these days,
   go fast and far.
Dreams are young, these days,
   or very old,
They can be black
   or blue or gold.
They need no special charts,
   nor any fuel.
It seems, only one rule applies,
   to all our dreams—
They will not fly except in open sky.
   A fenced-in dream
      will die.

Tests About Poetry

Multiple-Choice Test

When you take a multiple-choice test, you can think about the choices to be sure that you choose the best ones. Read the poem and then answer the questions that follow in the left column. Then, in the right column, read some ways you might think about the choices in questions 1–4.

> ## A Summer Morning
> by Rachel Field
>
> I saw dawn creep across the sky,
> And all the gulls go flying by.
> I saw the sea put on its dress
> Of blue midsummer loveliness,
> And heard the trees begin to stir
> Green arms of pine and juniper.
> I heard the wind call out and say:
> "Get up, my dear, it is today!"

Test Question	Answering the Question

1. What is the tone of the poem?
  A sad
  B angry
  C pleased
  D worried
	Question 1 There are really no sad or angry words, so answers *A* and *B* are not correct. Also, the speaker doesn't seem to be worried about anything, because he or she is just experiencing the *loveliness* of the morning, so answer *D* is not the best answer. The speaker's images of nature and the wind waking him or her up with the line *it is today* suggest that the speaker is pleased to be starting a new day, so *C* must be the best answer.

Test Question	Answering the Question
2. Which poetic device does the poet use in the phrase *I saw the sea put on its dress?* **A** simile **B** personification **C** metaphor **D** alliteration	**Question 2** There is no comparison in the quoted phrase, either with the words *like* or *as* or without them, so answers *A* (simile) and *C* (metaphor) are not correct. There is no alliteration, or repetition of initial consonant sounds, so answer *D* is not correct. But talking about the sea putting on a dress is giving the sea a human trait, so answer *B* (personification) must be correct.
3. The lines *I saw dawn creep across the sky* and *And all the gulls go flying by* provide an example of which poetic device? **A** onomatopoeia **B** exaggeration **C** idiom **D** rhyme	**Question 3** There aren't any words that sound like their meanings, so answer *A* (onomatopoeia) in not correct. There isn't really a good example of an idiom, or a phrase with a special meaning, in the poem, so answer *C* is not correct. The coming of dawn and the gulls flying are not exaggerating anything you would normally see, so answer *B* (exaggeration) is not the best answer. But the words *sky* and *by* do rhyme, or share the same ending sound, so answer *D* (rhyme) must be correct.
4. How do the combination of images—the sea, the trees, and the wind—contribute to the speaker's feeling about the new day? **A** They anger the speaker. **B** The speaker is still dreaming because the wind can't talk. **C** They give the speaker a peaceful feeling. **D** They are too noisy.	**Question 4** The speaker doesn't seem angry at being awakened *too early,* so *A* is not correct. The speaker is awake while experiencing his or her surroundings, so *B* is not correct. The trees and the wind seem pleasing to the speaker, so *D* is not correct. The words *loveliness* and *my dear* indicate a peaceful feeling, so *C* is the best answer.

Writing Test

Read the poem and then follow the directions to write your responses. When you write answers to a test question, you can think about your answers to be sure that they express your understanding. In the right column are some ways you might think about questions 5–7. (Some answers have been filled in as examples.)

74th Street
by Myra Cohn Livingston

Hey, this little kid gets roller skates.
She puts them on.
She stands up and almost
flops over backwards.
she sticks out a foot like
she's going somewhere and
falls down and
smacks her hand. She
grabs hold of a step to get up and
sticks out the other foot and
slides about six inches and
falls and
skins her knee.
          And then you know what?
She brushes off the dirt and the
blood and puts some
spit on it and then
sticks out the other foot
    again.

Test Question

5. List the action words from the poem that describe the skater's progress. Then add words of your own that describe how she must be feeling.

Action words
flops, falls, smacks, slides, skins
Words to Describe the Skater's Feelings
frustrated, tired, happy

Answering the Question

Question 5 Do the action words you have chosen all come from the poem? Are there any action words in the poem that you haven't listed?

Test Question	Answering the Question
6. Write three words of your own to describe the kind of person you think the skater is. | brave | strong | determined |	**Question 6** Do your words honestly express how you feel about the skater? Can you support them with examples from the poem?
7. Write a paragraph to a friend of yours. Describe the skater and her efforts to learn to skate. Then explain how you feel about the speaker and why. Use examples from the poem to support your answer.	**Question 7** Read the question carefully to be sure you understand what you are to write. Do you admire how the skater never gives up? Have you explained your feelings? Have you given reasons for the way you feel?